Cover design by: Joe De Leon

ISBN: 978-1-954089-62-4   1 2 3 4 5 6 7 8 9 10

PILOT

PREPARING INTEGRAL LEADERS OF TOMORROW

NICHOLAS JOHN

STUDY GUIDE

INSPIRE

CONTENTS

Chapter 1. The Journey Towards PILOT 6

Chapter 2. Preparing Yourself Well to Lead Well 12

Chapter 3. Preparing Yourself and Your
Significant Others 18

Chapter 4. If You Have Integrity, You Have Everything. 24

Chapter 5. Leaders Can Be Made 30

Chapter 6. Building Blocks for Future Leaders 36

Chapter 7. Tomorrow's Leaders Will Change the World
With Their Hearts 42

Chapter 8. Leading a Meaningful and Purposeful Life
as a Leader of Tomorrow 48

PILOT

PREPARING INTEGRAL LEADERS OF TOMORROW

NICHOLAS JOHN

chapter 1

THE JOURNEY TOWARDS PILOT

*Genuine leadership comes from the heart.
If you want to develop as a leader, then you
need to first develop or change your heart.*

Reading Time

Read Chapter 1: "The Journey Towards PILOT," in *PILOT*, reflect on the questions and discuss your answers with your study group.

REVIEW, REFLECT, AND RESPOND:

What has been one of the most important lessons you've learned throughout your leadership journey?

_____

_____

_____

_____

_____

_____

_____

_____

_____

What is the biggest obstacle you're struggling with now in your leadership or organizational life?

_____

_____

_____

_____

_____

_____

_____

_____

_____

_____

Consider the scripture above and answer the following questions:

What do you think the phrase from Luke 1:37, "For with God nothing will be impossible," meant to Mary?

_____

_____

_____

_____

_____

_____

How is this still applicable in our own lives and/or leadership today?

_____

_____

_____

_____

_____

_____

What does leadership mean to you? What does someone who leads
well look like?

_____

_____

_____

_____

_____

_____

_____

How are you intentionally investing in both your leadership
capability and those of the leaders of tomorrow?

_____

_____

_____

_____

_____

_____

Do you think humility is a trait that is essential in leadership?
Why or why not?

_____

_____

_____

_____

_____

_____

What do you base your leadership on? What do you use as a foundation and standard? How are you measuring up?

_____

_____

_____

_____

_____

_____

_____

_____

_____

_____

What prompted you to become a leader? How have you seen God use circumstances in your life to prepare you for your leadership role?

_____

_____

_____

_____

_____

_____

_____

_____

_____

_____

chapter 2

PREPARING YOURSELF WELL TO LEAD WELL

Preparing is the most vital part in any journey.

Reading Time

Read Chapter 2: "Preparing Yourself Well to Lead Well," in *PILOT*, reflect on the questions and discuss your answers with your study group.

REVIEW, REFLECT, AND RESPOND:

What steps of preparation have you taken of your own accord to ensure your leadership is effective?

_____

_____

_____

_____

_____

_____

_____

_____

_____

Do you think preparing is essential if a person wants to lead well? Why or why not?

_____

_____

_____

_____

_____

_____

_____

_____

_____

_____

Reflect on

Do not give dogs what is sacred; do not throw your pearls to pigs. If you do, they may trample them under their feet, and turn and tear you to pieces.

—Matthew 7:6 (NIV)

Consider the scripture above and answer the following questions:

What's your interpretation of Matthew 7:6?

_____

_____

_____

_____

_____

_____

_____

_____

How does this translate to a person's leadership?

_____

_____

_____

_____

_____

_____

_____

Have you ever not prepared for something, and it went horribly? Why was this the case? What would you do differently next time?

_____

_____

_____

_____

_____

_____

_____

_____

_____

_____

Do you think preparation alone can make or break a journey? Why or why not?

_____

_____

_____

_____

_____

_____

_____

_____

_____

_____

What revelations from Moses' divine calling to leadership did you draw from this chapter?

_____

_____

_____

_____

_____

_____

What obstacles that Moses overcame relate to something you struggle with in your leadership?

_____

_____

_____

_____

_____

_____

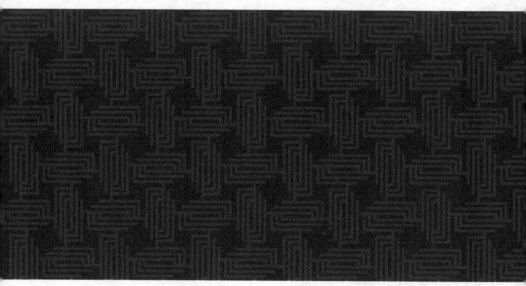

What's the difference between preparing and planning? Which has been more important to your outcomes?

_____

_____

_____

_____

_____

_____

_____

Why is finding out your WHO and WHY essential in the preparation process?

_____

_____

_____

_____

_____

_____

_____

chapter 3

PREPARING YOURSELF AND YOUR SIGNIFICANT OTHERS

For a leader's journey to be successful, the process of preparing will also need to extend to certain significant others.

REVIEW, REFLECT, AND RESPOND:

Do you think pain is inevitable in leadership? Why or why not?

_____

_____

_____

_____

_____

_____

When has your organization—or another organization you are aware of—advanced and someone on staff wasn't able to stay effective? What happened in that situation?

_____

_____

_____

_____

_____

_____

_____

_____

_____

_____

_____

_____

Reflect on

I consider that our present sufferings are not worth comparing with the glory that will be revealed in us.

—Romans 8:18 (NIV)

Consider the scripture above and answer the following questions:

How is Romans 8:18 applicable to leadership?

_____

_____

_____

_____

_____

_____

_____

How would you encourage someone who is discouraged by his or her leadership sufferings?

_____

_____

_____

_____

_____

_____

_____

_____

Is preparation an act or an ongoing process? Explain your answer.

_____

_____

_____

_____

_____

_____

_____

Of the areas of preparation discussed in this chapter, which do you most need to incorporate into your preparation? Why?

_____

_____

_____

_____

_____

_____

What happens if those supporting us aren't ready to advance to what is next? How can you ensure that they are ready?

_____

_____

_____

_____

_____

_____

_____

_____

How does focusing on the promise help us overcome the pain?

_____

_____

_____

_____

_____

_____

_____

Of the following: work, family, health, friends, and spirit, which do you tend to overprioritize? Which do you not give enough attention to? What do each of those situations look like?

_____

_____

_____

_____

_____

_____

_____

_____

_____

_____

_____

_____

_____

_____

_____

_____

chapter 4

IF YOU HAVE INTEGRITY, YOU HAVE EVERYTHING

Integrity is a quality you can't fake.

REVIEW, REFLECT, AND RESPOND:

Why is integrity important in leadership? What happens if a leader has no integrity?

_____

_____

_____

_____

_____

_____

_____

_____

_____

Why do you consider yourself a leader of integrity? Would those who work closely with you say the same?

_____

_____

_____

_____

_____

_____

_____

_____

_____

_____

_____

Consider the scripture above and answer the following questions:

What does Proverbs 11:4 mean when it speaks of righteousness?

_____

_____

_____

_____

_____

_____

Are we able to be righteous in our own power? If not, how should a person go about getting righteousness?

_____

_____

_____

_____

_____

_____

_____

_____

_____

Have you ever worked under a leader who didn't have integrity? What was the result?

_____

_____

_____

_____

_____

Why is it important to "guard our integrity daily"? What happens if people aren't intentional in this process?

_____

_____

_____

_____

_____

_____

_____

_____

_____

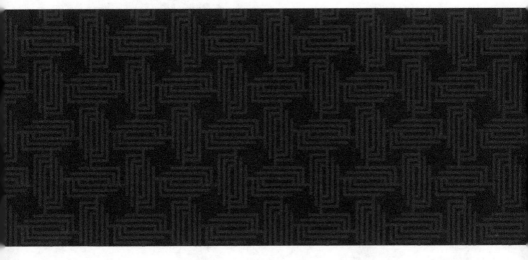

How do you find yourself compartmentalizing your life when it comes to scrutinizing your integrity? What parts of your life get separated from the rest?

_____

_____

_____

_____

_____

_____

_____

How are integrity and trust connected? How do they add to or subtract from one another? Explain your answers.

_____

_____

_____

_____

_____

_____

_____

_____

_____

_____

Of the different proverbs listed in Chapter 4 that relate to integrity, which stands out to you and why? What is the meaning of the proverb you chose?

_____

_____

_____

_____

_____

_____

_____

_____

_____

_____

_____

_____

_____

_____

_____

chapter 5

LEADERS CAN BE MADE

Leaders can be made like bread is made. But this process of making a leader is not an easy one!

REVIEW, REFLECT, AND RESPOND:

How long does it take for a leader to develop? What determines the length of the process?

_____

_____

_____

_____

_____

_____

_____

_____

Why do you think it's important for leaders to be intentional in their growth and development?

_____

_____

_____

_____

_____

_____

_____

_____

_____

_____

Reflect on

Now the overseer is to be above reproach, faithful to his wife, temperate, self-controlled, respectable, hospitable, able to teach, not given to drunkenness, not violent but gentle, not quarrelsome, not a lover of money. He must manage his own family well and see that his children obey him, and he must do so in a manner worthy of full respect.

—1 Timothy 3:2-4 (NIV)

Consider the scripture above and answer the following questions:

What stands out to you about the standards listed?

_____

_____

_____

_____

How do you and the leaders you know stand up to them?

_____

_____

_____

_____

What impact do those standards make on one's ability to lead others?

_____

_____

_____

_____

What kind of people aren't capable of being leaders? What disqualifies them?

_____

_____

_____

_____

_____

_____

_____

_____

_____

Of the DNA for future leaders, which ingredient do you think is the most important? Why?

_____

_____

_____

_____

_____

What would you say to someone who says leaders are born—not made? Why is this statement inaccurate?

_____

_____

_____

_____

_____

_____

Is there a place for love in leadership? How does a leader who loves those he or she leads express that love in an appropriate and effective way?

_____

_____

_____

_____

_____

_____

_____

_____

_____

Why is it important for leaders to admit their mistakes? What kind of culture does this promote within an organization?

_____

_____

_____

_____

_____

_____

_____

_____

_____

_____

chapter 6

BUILDING BLOCKS FOR FUTURE LEADERS

Now more than ever, we need moral leaders to impact and influence our world. You can be one of these leaders.

REVIEW, REFLECT, AND RESPOND:

What is the most effective foundation for leaders? What should leaders base their other building blocks on?

_____

_____

_____

_____

_____

_____

_____

_____

What does it mean to listen versus to hear? What's the difference, and when should we be utilizing each?

_____

_____

_____

_____

_____

_____

_____

_____

_____

Reflect on

Trust in the LORD with all thine heart; and lean not unto thine own understanding.

—Proverbs 3:5-6 (NKJV)

Consider the scripture above and answer the following questions:

What does Proverbs 3:5-6 mean when it says, "In all thy ways acknowledge him"?

_____

_____

_____

_____

_____

_____

_____

_____

What does it mean to actually do this in our lives and leadership?

_____

_____

_____

_____

_____

_____

_____

_____

_____

Do you think questions are important to ask in communication, decision-making, and conflict management? Why or why not?

_____

_____

_____

_____

_____

_____

_____

_____

How can you be more intentional in your communication? In what area of communication do you lack? How can you strengthen it?

_____

_____

_____

_____

_____

_____

_____

_____

_____

_____

_____

_____

_____

How can we be sure we're making the right decisions? What decision-making process does your organization utilize when making big choices?

_____

_____

_____

_____

_____

_____

_____

_____

_____

_____

_____

_____

How effective are you at managing conflict? How long does it take you to handle conflict when it arises?

_____

_____

_____

_____

_____

_____

_____

_____

_____

_____

_____

_____

_____

Why is it not possible to avoid conflict? What happens if we are experiencing no conflict in our lives?

_____

_____

_____

_____

_____

_____

_____

_____

_____

_____

_____

_____

_____

_____

chapter 7

TOMORROW'S LEADERS WILL CHANGE THE WORLD WITH THEIR HEARTS

It's my desire for tomorrow's leaders all over the world to begin developing their hearts.

Read Chapter 7: "Tomorrow's Leaders Will Change the World With Their Hearts," in *PILOT*, reflect on the questions and discuss your answers with your study group.

REVIEW, REFLECT, AND RESPOND:

Why is it important for us to pour into the leaders of tomorrow's world?

_____

_____

_____

_____

_____

_____

_____

_____

_____

How can we as leaders stay effective amid all the change that is currently going on around us and in society?

_____

_____

_____

_____

_____

_____

_____

_____

_____

Reflect on

Moses' father-in-law replied, "What you are doing is not good. You and these people who come to you will only wear yourselves out. The work is too heavy for you; you cannot handle it alone."

—Exodus 18:17-18 (NIV)

Consider the scripture above and answer the following questions:

What's important about what Jethro said to his son-in-law Moses?

_____

_____

_____

_____

When might this be applicable to us as leaders, too?

_____

_____

_____

_____

How would you go about counseling a leader in Moses' position?

_____

_____

_____

_____

How do you define execution? What's the most important factor in getting something done?

_____

_____

_____

_____

_____

_____

_____

_____

_____

_____

When it comes to choosing your team, what are some steps you can take to ensure you're hiring the right fit?

_____

_____

_____

_____

_____

_____

_____

_____

_____

_____

_____

_____

What happens if we aren't intentional about adapting and staying effective? Can we still achieve what we set out to do?

_____

_____

_____

_____

_____

_____

_____

_____

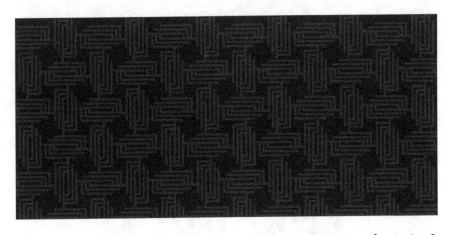

How can sin inhibit our leadership and our organizational mission?

_____

_____

_____

_____

_____

_____

_____

What does it mean to be a "Conscious Leader"? What are the advantages of conscious leadership?

_____

_____

_____

_____

_____

_____

_____

_____

_____

chapter 8

LEADING A MEANINGFUL AND PURPOSEFUL LIFE AS A LEADER OF TOMORROW

You need to understand what your meaning and purpose as a leader will be, and that comes from understanding your WHO as a leader.

REVIEW, REFLECT, AND RESPOND:

What are some intentional steps we can take today to ensure we're effective leaders tomorrow?

_____

_____

_____

_____

_____

_____

_____

_____

Define potential in your own words. How does one achieve his or her potential in God? How easy is it?

_____

_____

_____

_____

_____

_____

_____

_____

_____

_____

Reflect on

My frame was not hidden from You,
When I was made in secret,
And skillfully wrought in the lowest parts of the earth.
Your eyes saw my substance, being yet unformed.
And in Your book they all were written,
The days fashioned for me,
When as yet there were none of them.

—Psalm 139:15-16 (NKJV)

Consider the scripture above and answer the following questions:

What does Psalm 139:15-16 say about God's involvement in each person's unique creation and His plans for their lives?

_____

_____

_____

_____

_____

_____

How might embracing these verses affect how people lead and others follow?

_____

_____

_____

_____

_____

_____

_____

What is your meaning and purpose in life and as a leader? Explain your answer.

_____

_____

_____

_____

_____

_____

_____

_____

The DREAM acronym equips people to find their meaning and purpose. What step of this process do you need to be more deliberate about? What is your plan for making that happen?

_____

_____

_____

_____

_____

_____

_____

_____

_____

_____

_____

What are the "turkeys"—or distractions—in your life? How can you deliberately remove them?

_____

_____

_____

_____

_____

_____

_____

_____

_____

_____

_____

Who do you know struggles to keep a positive attitude in the face of opposition? Why do you think this is, and how might you encourage that person?

_____

_____

_____

_____

_____

_____

_____

_____

_____

_____

_____

_____

_____

_____

_____

_____

Do you fully believe that with God on your side, anything is possible? Do you trust in the possibility of your dreams through Him?

_____

_____

_____

_____

_____

_____

_____

_____

_____

_____

_____

_____

_____

CPSIA information can be obtained
at www.ICGtesting.com
Printed in the USA
BVHW041952280921
617616BV00022B/875